Natascha **Snelder-Bouman**

the **Parrot**

A guide to selection, care, housing,

nutrition, behaviour, health and breeding

Contents

Foreword

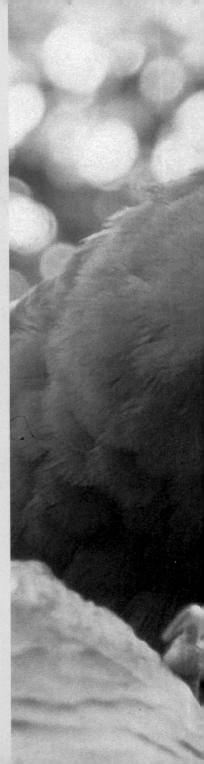

In many countries, the number of exotic birds kept as pets is increasing, especially tropical birds, which we cannot find in the wild in our Northern European climate. The breeding of exotic birds has advanced so far that it is no longer necessary to catch them from the rainforest, whether legally or illegally, and to ship them to enthusiasts all over the world. Almost all types are bred successfully in captivity. This prevents a lot of stress, adjustment problems and the death of birds, which did not survive the journey.

Pakara is a bird society in the Netherlands and Belgium that specialises in the keeping, looking after and breeding of bigger parrots, Amazons, cockatoos and macaws. The most important goal is to ensure the welfare of the big parrots, both in captivity and the wild. A 'wildling', as described above, is therefore against our goals. Pakara is approached by many people, who have questions about their hobby, and has been happy to cooperate with the About Pets team in developing this book.

The writer has certainly hit the nail on the head with this book, and it is therefore highly recommended. This book is worth the money you have paid for it many times over. It offers both new and experienced enthusiasts advice that helps both the bird and the owner. It is intended for people who want to know more about the parrot they purchased or rather (preferably) about the parrot they intend to buy. The saying "think before you begin" certainly applies when you're thinking of acquiring a parrot.

I wish you much pleasure, both with this book and, of course, with your bird(s). It is and always will be a fantastic hobby!

Aad van Duyneveldt
Chairman Pakara

Copyright © 2003
About Pets
co-publisher United Kingdom
Kingdom Books
PO9 5TL, England

ISBN 185279206X
First printing
September 2003

Original title: *de Papegaai*
© 2001 - 2003 Welzo Media Productions bv,
Warffum, the Netherlands
http://www.overdieren.nl

Photos:
Pakara, Natascha Snelder,
Rob Dekker and
Rob Doolaard

Printed in Italy

In general

Larger parrot types are found on all continents and south of the equator. There are more than 300 different types.

African Grey Congo
(Psittacus erithacus)

They vary in length from 10 to 100 centimetres. They also vary in colour, mobility, sound volume, habitat and behaviour. Sadly, the number of parrot types is still decreasing due to illegal hunting, destruction of their habitat and possible nesting places, and other reasons, all of which are man-made.

Western man was fascinated by the parrot family ever since it was brought back to cold Europe by explorers. Sometimes this attraction has been fatal for the wild birds.

All domesticated parrots learn very quickly how to get what they want. A rigorous, yet friendly upbringing is important to prevent birds becoming spoiled animals,

which only seek attention by screaming and biting.

A lot of parrots are kept in this country and enjoy living in the company of humans. You will find advice on feeding, behaviour, housing and other demands these beautiful birds have. This book has been written to help you and your bird enjoy each other's company.

Senegal Parrot
(Poicephalus senegalus)

Buying a Parrot

You've decided that a parrot fits with your present and future lifestyle and you want to purchase a (young) bird.

Red-lored Amazon
(*Amazona autumnalis*)

How can you make sure that the bird you are choosing is healthy, fits in with your way of life and that it will give you pleasure for many years to come? Here are some tips:

• Keep your eyes open when buying and try to keep your heart and emotions at bay. Only buy a completely independent bird. Do not start with baby-feeding your first chick to raise it to independence. And only buy a bird that your whole family likes.

• There is no on/off button on a parrot, so you have to be 300% sure that a parrot suits your lifestyle and vice versa, before you take on this responsibility. A parrot will return all the love and attention you give it many times over.

• Some people like to raise a chick by hand themselves, hoping to bond the bird to them and to tame it. There are plenty of chicks that have been raised adequately by their parents. These are just as suitable as pets, although it sometimes takes a bit more attention to get them tame.

• Never buy a young parrot which has to be hand-fed if you do not have any experience doing this! The bird will feed independently a few weeks later, and this is the right time to bring it home. The bird will not be less tame.

• There is a big difference between imported wild birds and pets that have been raised at a breeder's. Most types are bred in sufficient numbers in this country. It is therefore not necessary to catch wild birds and it is not advisable to buy such birds.

These birds are so traumatised by the journey that they often cannot get over this experience. They can often not be tamed afterwards.
• Always keep in mind that these birds easily reach an average age of 35.

Choosing a young bird

You have to bear several things in mind when choosing a young bird. The first point to consider is the bird's breeder. The future relationship has to be based on empathy and communication between buyer and breeder. Get plenty of advice from experts who can recommend a good breeder. Ask a lot of questions about anything you can think of and you want to know more about. A good breeder will be happy to tell you everything and more. Ask to see the parent animals. It is best to see the parents and the young together. You can then be sure that this breeder bred the bird in question.

Do not take the bird home after you have seen it for the first time. Give yourself time to think it over (however difficult that may be) and make a new appointment with the breeder when you are sure that you want to buy the bird. When you go to pick the bird up, take some of the food that the breeder fed it. You can use this for the first few days. You may then change the food. The bird's price is an important thing to consider when buying. Parrots are an expensive purchase, and this is not all. You also have to have some money for the housing and the food. By looking at potential cages and aviaries, you will have a better idea about the total costs.

Eclectus parrot female
(Eclectus roratus)

A healthy parrot should not:
• crouch with its feathers standing up
• constantly sleep while people are standing in front of its cage
• breathe in gasps or wheezes
• let its tale whip in the rhythm of its breathing
• let its wings droop
• have lice or feather mites on or under its feathers
• sleep on the ground
• show bald patches

A healthy parrot should:
• have fine plumage, which lies smoothly against the body
• clean its feathers regularly
• have shiny eyes
• have dry nostrils without discharge or crusts
• keep its beak closed when resting
• keep an eye on its surroundings
• have a clean anus
• eat independently
• sit on a perch and sleep on one leg (young birds on two!)
• have a smooth and clean beak

Yellow-crowned Parrot *(Amazona ochrocephala)*

Sulphur Crested
Cockatoo *(Cacatua
sulphure amazone)*

Blue-fronted
Amazon
(Amazona aestiva)

Identification

When you are buying a parrot, make sure that it has a solid identification ring to show that it has been bred in captivity. This is very important at the moment, as the laws about exotic species are becoming stricter. A solid identification ring can only be put on chicks. It usually displays a unique number, which identifies the breeder, the year of birth and another number. The solid identification ring is the only proof that a bird has been bred in captivity and has not been imported from the rainforest.

U-rings are rings that are not completely closed. They can therefore also be put on grown birds. These rings are therefore no proof that a bird was born in captivity. A ring on the left or right leg does not indicate the sex, although this is often assumed. An electronic

chip is also a very good method of identification. A chip can also be implanted in a grown bird and is therefore no proof of birth in captivity. A chip is, however, useful in case of escape or theft. A chip cannot be removed, whereas an identification ring can.

The avian veterinarian

We advise you to make an agreement with the breeder about having the bird checked by a vet specialised in birds. The avian veterinarian can examine the bird(s) for evaluation and checks. In agreement with the vet, you can discuss which tests should be done during such a 'vetting'.

Purchase contract

To prevent disappointments and misunderstandings, it is important that agreements with the breeder are in writing. This can be a purchase contract, where you can mention the following: details of buyer and breeder; ring number and maybe chip number of the bird; species; details of the vetting; agreed tests; key conditions of the purchase, share of costs of possible examinations.

Yellow-crowned Parrot *(Amazona ochrocephala)*

Eclectus Parrots *(Eclectus roratus)*

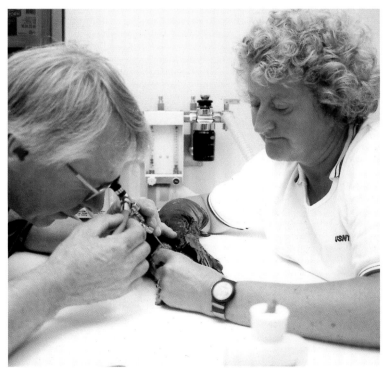

An avian veterinarian preforming a laparoscopy in order to determine the sex of an individual bird. Here, the veterinarian is inserting the laparoscope trocar into the bird.

Greater Vasa Parrot
(Coracopsis vasa)

St. Vincent Amazon
(Amazona guildingi)

Quarantine

If you already have birds, you should keep the new bird apart for a while. You can then observe the bird and wait for the test results. The new bird can get used to its new surroundings. Getting it used to new food is also easier this way. Your existing group of birds will not be at risk in case the new one does after all appear to have a disease. The minimum quarantine period is 6 weeks.

DEFRA

Most parrot species are successfully bred in captivity. It is no longer necessary to import these species to Europe from the wild. It is also forbidden to catch many species in the wild. If you do want to do this, it is often very expensive.

All parrot species, apart from the Budgerigar and the Cockatiel, are currently protected under the law for endangered foreign animal and plant species. You must to have a licence to keep rare species. For more common species, this means that you may only keep them if you can prove that the individual bird has been bred in captivity (with some exceptions). The solid identification ring proves this.

If you already have a parrot in your home, and it does not have a solid identification ring, you have to prove that you owned this bird before the 1st of August 1995. If you can bring this proof, then it is possible to get a licence via the Defra. You have to contact the Defra before transporting or selling a bird.

Department for Environment Food and Rural Affairs (Defra)
Wildlife Licensing Section
Global Wildlife Division
1/17 Temple Quay House
2 The Square
Temple Quay
Bristol
BS1 6EB
www.defra.gov.uk

In general, it is advisable to only choose a ringed bird when buying a new bird. You can check whether you need to have any other licences with the Defra bureau. Parrots need very intensive care and lots of attention, even if they live with us. Some species are therefore not suitable as pets.

Orange-winged Amazon (*Amazona amazonica*)

Feeding your parrot

The issue of feeding is a favourite topic in conversations between parrot owners. The one honestly reveals how he mixes his seed mixture.

The other prefers to keep his secret recipe to himself. Number three even gives his birds 'pellets' or dry food, just as dogs and cats are fed. One thing is certain: there are as many tastes as there are birds. Just as with people, parrots have their own character and their own likes and dislikes when it comes to food. Every pet shop sells parrot food. These include seed mixes, egg food, conditioning and growth food, grit, buds, stomach gravel and 'responsible parrot treats'. The number of pellet foods on the market has increased over the last few years.

It is down to each owner to chose a menu for his darling(s). It is important that it results in a balanced and plentiful diet so that the bird can grow old in good health.

A good, healthy feeding forms the basis for optimum care and the well-being of the bird.

'Traditional' feeds

Everybody knows the ready-made seed mixtures sold in pet shops. One mix has more sunflower seeds, the other has less peanuts. In any case, the mixture contains seeds of various sizes, nuts and maybe peanuts.

When choosing a mixture, the amount of sunflower seeds is vital. Sunflower seeds are very fattening and have only very little nutritional value. You can raise the nutritional value of a mix with too many sunflower seeds by mixing in other seeds and nuts. You also have to be careful with peanuts in shells. These contain poisonous aflatoxins and are also very fattening, If you do want to feed peanuts, it is better to buy the roasted variety intended for human consumption. They fulfil higher quality demands, but they are still very fattening!

Vital necessity

Food is the most vital element in a parrot's life, too. Unbalanced feeding leads to deficiencies, poor condition or bad breeding results. Until a few years ago, the nutritional requirements of parrots had not been examined very closely. Luckily, this has changed in the last decade, and parrot enthusiasts benefit from this. A good, healthy feeding is the basis for optimum care and the well-being of the bird.

Possible deficiencies, which can be caused by bad or unilateral feeding:
- lack of protein; unbalanced protein percentage; lack of essential amino acids (lysine, methionine, and others)
- lack of vitamins (A, D, E, K, and others)
- lack of minerals (calcium, phosphorus, sodium, and others)
- lack of trace elements (iodine, manganese, selenium, and others)

On the basis of experience, discussions with other enthusiasts, reading and trial & error, everybody finds their own menu composition. It takes a long time and a lot of experimenting (and asking) before a bird has the right menu.

Alternative feeds: parrot pellets

Some manufacturers have brought pellets for parrots on the market. These pellets have been made by extrusion. Due to extreme heating (to about 200 °C), these pellets are free of bacteria.

Pellets are most commonly used for chickens, pigeons, dogs, cats and horses. They are not yet very popular for parrots. Some manufacturers make pellets for all parrot species; others have different types of pellets - depending on the needs of a certain species or the time of the year (resting or breeding time).

Buru Racket-tailed Parrot *(Prioniturus mada)*

Advantages of pellets:
- the bird gets the right amount of nutrients with each bite
- easy to feed, even when someone else is looking after the bird
- less mess

Disadvantages of pellets:
- boring for the owner
- bird has less variety to choose from
- not always easy to get

Everybody has to make his own decisions for his bird. Always be aware that your parrot is intelligent and has its preferences.
When given a bowl with various seeds and nuts, it will begin with the tastiest (and most fattening), and throw the rest out. When given new food regularly, it will only eat the fattening, tastiest things. Anything you give your

Red-tailed Cockatoo female *(Calyptorhynchus magnificus)*

Black-headed
Caique *(Pionites
melanocephala)*

White-bellied
Caique *(Pionites
leucogaster)*

parrot has to be within limits and with thought. It is not a question of your bird finishing off its bowl, including the small, not quite so tasty morsels. Those are usually the healthiest! Pellets seem boring, but your bird should not search for distraction via its food. Attention from people around it, toys, tasks and other such things must provide distraction - not the food, no matter what is in the bowl!

Also on the menu

It is important that you offer your parrot further variety in its food. Besides products from pet shops and vets, there are plenty of

every-day foods that your parrot will enjoy.

Vegetables and fruit

Parrots like all vegetables and fruit, apart from the highly poisonous (for parrots) avocado. Apple, pear, carrot, paprika, lettuce, cabbage, broccoli, mango, anything can be fed. Soft fruits, such as bananas, mandarins, strawberries, cherries or grapes probably do not cross your mind straight away, but most parrots love them. Rose hips are also popular. They grow in the wild in many places. Freeze them and later defrost, wash and feed them to your birds during the course of the year. The same

applies to sweetcorn. Make sure that you do not collect rose hips and sweetcorn beside busy roads, as they will be polluted. Do not be shocked if your bird has red droppings after you fed it a cherry or strawberry. This really scared me the first time it happened, until I remembered the cherries.

Nuts

All parrots love nuts. Big macaws and cockatoos can crack a lot of nuts themselves. Smaller parrot species prefer it if you open the nuts for them. All nuts are suitable. Be aware of what I mentioned earlier about peanut shells and make sure that there is no mould

on the nuts. By cracking the nuts, you can check them inside and look for mould.

Hard-boiled eggs

My birds are fed these once a week, peeled, instead of ready-made egg-food. Once a month, they also get a piece of fresh garlic with their eggs. This gets rid of any possible worms and is very healthy for a parrot. The birds smell from all pores for a few hours.

Natural yoghurt

This is (in a limited amount) good for the intestinal flora. If your birds find it too sharp, you can

Hawk-headed Parrot *(Deroptyus accipitrinus)*

mix a banana in or add a little rose hip marmalade or juice.

Muesli

Tasty with a little milk, yoghurt or fruit juice.

Sprouts

A number of seed, pods and beans are suitable for sprouting. Put the seeds in a flat bowl with water to soften. Rinse them several times and let the seeds sprout on some damp kitchen roll for 24 hours. As soon as small white/ green sprouts become visible, you can feed them to your bird. Especially in the spring, this is an ideal supplement for your birds, which are ready to breed. Softened seeds, pods and beans, which have been soaked in water, are also very popular.

Grit and stomach gravel

This is very good for your bird's digestive system.

Besides its food, your parrot always has to have fresh drinking water!

Feed and heat

It is important to regularly change all soft food regularly on hot summer days, in order to prevent mould. The cage also requires more attention than usual. Birds excrete a lot, and mould and bacteria develop on the floor quicker in the heat.

Hawk-headed Parrot *(Deroptyus accipitrinus)*

Out of the question!

Parrots do not eat or drink things such as (salty) crisps, chips, coffee, tea, alcohol and chocolate in the wild. Therefore also feed your domesticated animals natural food for good health. The above items should never be fed to a bird, however much your bird likes a pint! You can read more on poisonous and dangerous situations in the chapter 'dangers in the house'.

Feeding chicks

As this book is addressed to parrot enthusiasts, and as I am against the purchase of still dependent chicks by inexperienced owners, this subject will not be discussed further. I advise any enthusiast wanting a young bird to delay with the purchase until the bird can eat by itself. This means that it has to be able to peel all its seeds, nuts, peanuts and so on, and has to be able to eat solid food. A young parrot is independent at a few months. The precise age varies from species to species.

Hyacinthine Macaw *(Anodorhynchus hyacinthinus)*

A home for your parrot

The bigger the cage or aviary, the better, as any cage or aviary is in fact too small. As everybody has to make do with the limitations of their house, garden or garage, one has to choose.

Red-lored
Amazon
*(Amazona
autumnalis)*

This means that it is important to know what sorts of demands the different species have in terms of their habitat. A macaw needs a different home than a Senegal parrot. It is also important for your neighbours what type of cage you choose and what species (with the accompanying volume) you keep. Get plenty of information about the needs of your chosen variety from the breeder(s). Be careful when selecting the home for your birds and ask, ask, ask.

Generally speaking, the following cage types are available for parrots:
• cage
• indoor aviary
• aviary outdoors with or without hut
• flight

Cages
Cages are available in many colours, sizes and designs. Cages can stand on wheels, on four legs or a single foot. Choose a strong, reliable design and avoid cages with a round top. These are not suitable for parrots, as they like to climb. A square or rectangular cage offers far more opportunities for climbing.

Make sure that the bars can with-stand the parrot's beak and run horizontally, so that the bird can climb on them. Also make sure that no dangerous pieces stick out that could injure the bird. Make sure that the cage is big enough for your bird and regularly check the bars for any irregularities. Also ensure that the bird cannot open the cage itself. A bird can get stuck if the distances between the bars are too big, it can injure itself on sharp edges or escape through irregular bars. Some cages have sharp edges when the door is opened.

A pull-out floor tray is easy to clean. A lot of cages have a separate open grid on the floor. The opinions about these vary widely. Arguments for such a grid are that the excretions and the food remnants fall through the grid, so that the bird itself remains clean when it walks over it. Disadvantages are that it requires a lot of cleaning, as excretion sticks to the bars, and walking over the grid is very uncomfortable for the bird. It can also damage its tail feathers on the grid. A cage with a 'soft roof' (for example an oilcloth) can be helpful if the bird flies against the roof in panic. Some cages can be opened at the top. The roof is folded open to both sides, and an extra perch is placed on top. It is an ideal observation spot for the bird when it is allowed to fly free.

Perches that come with the cage usually all have the same length and circumference. This is handy, but it is better for the bird to replace them with natural sticks, which you can cut to size. This stimulates your bird's claws, as it will always have to adjust them instead of always having the same position.

Put the (indoor) cage in a quiet place, but one where your parrot can take part in family life. A parrot is prey in the wild, and therefore prefers to have a wall behind it, so that no danger can come from behind. A spot at the window is not suitable because of draughts and the risk of too much heat if the bird is standing in the sun. You might want to install a night-lamp, so that it does not get completely dark, and the bird can orientate itself should it be frightened.

Second-hand cages

Cages and aviaries are expensive to purchase, but last a long time. If you decide to get a second-hand cage, do not immediately put a new bird in it, however clean it seems to be. It is better to disinfect the cage thoroughly with special solutions, which you can buy in the pet shop. After that, you need to clean the cage thoroughly with hot water to get rid of all the remains of this (often very aggressive) product. Then you can prepare the cage for its new resident. Always follow the instructions on the disinfectant packaging.

Indoor aviary

If you have enough room, an indoor aviary is ideal. It is room-high, with a square or rectangular form. They are usually made of wire mesh. Make sure that the mesh is the right size. Indoor aviaries are also available in various

Yellow-collared Macaw
(Ara auricollis)

African Grey Congo
(Psittacus erithacus)

Muller's Parrot
*(Tanygnathus
sumatranus)*

Great-billed Parrot
*(Tanygnathus m.
Megalorhynchus)*

colours, on wheels or with little feet and they usually feature a pull-out floor tray for easy cleaning. For the interior of the aviary, the same points as for the cage and the general points listed below apply.

Outdoor aviary with or without hut

If you want to keep your birds in an aviary outdoors, you will again be faced with various designs and qualities. You can buy them ready-made, to assemble yourself, or you can build it yourself from scratch.

Some important points, which have not yet been mentioned:

• Many communities require a planning permission for the building. Find out yourself about the regulations where you live. If you need planning permission, it is important to ask for it as soon as possible so you can start the actual building when you planned to. When planning permission is requested for an aviary, many communities first check in the neighbourhood to see whether there are any objections. You can, of course, ask the neighbours about their opinion yourself. This can prevent a lot of trouble later.

• Vermin in an outdoor aviary can cause a lot of problems. You can prevent this for example by laying a good foundation under your aviary, and by not feeding outdoors if a hut is available.

• As our climate is not suitable to keep parrots outdoors all year round, a hut is necessary in an outdoor aviary. Via a flap the birds can decide whether to spend their time outside or inside. The flaps can be closed, so you can keep the birds inside in cold weather. Feeding and drinking bowls, and maybe the nesting boxes, are in the hut.

• You can use any empty space in a shed, garage or a part of the house, to which an outdoor aviary can be attached, as a hut. A connection to outdoors is established via tunnels in the wall.

Always keep an eye on the temperature for your birds. A parrot's delicate parts, such as the claws, can easily freeze. A heating (element) in the hut is a good solution. You can use various plants, weeds and shrubs to plant in the aviary. For advice on which plants are most suitable, we recommend you read specialist books or see your local gardener or garden centre.

A flight

A flight (an enormous aviary), in which the birds have enough space to fly longer distances, is the best approach for a natural situation. Sadly, this solution is reserved for the very few of us who have a large garden, for zoos and bird parks. We will therefore not go into this subject.

Suitable materials

Make sure that you use material of good quality. Larger parrot species, such as amazons, cockatoos and macaws, need aviaries with a

frame of (stainless) steel, zinc-coated or galvanised material. These are preferable to wood, which is often chewed on straight away. If you do want to use wood, cover it with mesh, so that the wood is protected. Get information on the right size of mesh and attach it firmly to the wood with pop rivets. Food and drink bowls can be attached in different ways: on a solid plateau in the cage or aviary, on a swivel plateau or just hanging loosely on the mesh. The bowls can be of plastic or stainless steel.

Cage litter

Old newspapers and a layer of sawdust or shavings are suitable for a cage. Sawdust causes a lot of dust; shavings are not as dusty. You can also use newspapers, woodshavings and sawdust in an indoor aviary. You can use sand, soil or concrete for an outdoor aviary.

Toys

Whether you are preparing a cage, an aviary or a flight for your parrots, they all like toys. Especially if a bird is only kept indoors, it is important to pay attention to such items. Anything put in the cage has to withstand the destructive power of a parrot's beak, and it must not contain poisonous substances. Especially with cockatoos and macaws, it is very important to use toys made of very good quality material. Otherwise they

Salmon-crested Cockatoo
(Cacatua moluccensis)

Jardine's Parrot
(Poicephalus gulielmi)

White-capped
Parrot
(Pionus Senilis)

Lilac-crowned
Amazon *(Amazona
finschi)*

will open the fastening within no time, and the toy will lie uselessly on the floor. Toys of good quality need not be expensive. A few thick ropes can quickly be turned into interesting climbing toys or swings.

Further furnishings

A cage or aviary also needs various bowls. They should be attached firmly. Bowls are necessary for water, food, fruit and vegetables and possibly for stomach grit. All bowls need to be washed out

daily. If the surrounding of your parrot is very dry, you can offer him a separate bath. Most birds enjoy splashing around a bit. This is very good for their feathers. Most birds also enjoy being sprayed with a plant sprayer or they might even like a shower. You must be extremely careful with draughts if the bird is sitting in its cage wet.

Twigs

All parrots like plenty of fresh twigs. Twigs of willow or of (unsprayed) fruit trees are ideal. It offers a tremendous distraction to the parrots and the twigs are converted into small splinters in no time. Breeding birds will use the splinters as a supplement to their nesting box. The twigs moisten the air in the box, which supports growth.

If you buy a couple, you can add a nesting box to the interior. You will find more information on breeding parrots in the chapter on this subject.

Chestnut-fronted Macaw
(Ara severa)

Dangers in the house

A bird in the house is a real gain. A parrot that is allowed to fly free for a few hours a day really enjoys it. However, accidents can happen. The following is a list with a few of the dangers that can threaten your bird in the domestic environment. We have listed descriptions of potential results and ways to prevent these dangers. Do not despair when reading the following list; it is intended as something to keep in mind in your daily care of your winged friend.

Glue, paint and lacquer

Glue, paint and/or lacquer can lead to fatal poisoning due to volatile substances. Remove all animals from rooms in which glue, paint or lacquer are being used and ventilate the room thoroughly after use. Builder's merchants, DIY stores and specialist stores can advise you on the use of certain substances and how to prevent damage to humans and animals alike.

Bathroom

Dangers in a bathroom include escape through an open window, drowning in an open toilet, a full sink, bucket or bathtub, poisoning through cleaning products or chemicals. The following applies: keep the bird away from bathrooms, or close all the windows before it is allowed in. Make sure that there are no full sinks, buckets or baths in the bathroom. Keep the lid on the toilet closed.

Goffin's Cockatoo
(Cacatua goffini)

Gaps

A parrot can easily get caught in gaps, for example between a wall and a cupboard. Being stuck often results in death through a heart

Chattering Lory
(Lorius garrulus)

Bodinus' Amazon
Amazona f. bodini

attack as the bird violently, but vainly, tries to free itself. It can also result in damage to wings and legs. Make sure that you leave no gaps when placing furniture.

Doors

Doors are dangerous to parrots, as they can get caught or crushed in them. A door (to the outdoors) also offers the opportunity to escape. Only great care can prevent this.

Draughts

Colds, pneumonia and even death are the potential results of draughts. Prevent these as far as

possible. Do not place the cage or aviary in a place where there is a draught. Be especially aware of draughts in summer when you open windows and/or doors.

Electric cables

The danger here is an electric shock by chewing and biting on or through cables. This can be fatal instantly. Hide electric cables or cover them with strips or hollow planks. Also remove plugs from sockets.

Kitchen

Overheated kitchens and the necessary ventilation lead to cold draughts, steam and gasses that attack the respiratory system, Teflon fumes (from non-stick pans) are lethal, and the parrot can also get burned on hot pots, pans and food. Do not keep birds in closed kitchens or ensure sufficient ventilation (beware of draughts). Do not leave hot pots and pans uncovered. Make sure that the bird cannot reach open bottles/pots.

Other birds
The dangers from other birds in the house are fight wounds through bigger or rivalling birds, and stress-development. Never let birds of different sizes together without supervision. Introduce new birds in separate cages first, then carefully put them together in the aviary and observe them well. You must also be careful with other pets.

Windows
Your bird can fly against a window and suffer concussion, a broken neck or internal injuries. Therefore cover glass (windows, balcony doors) with curtains or blinds and accustom the bird to the invisible barrier by opening the curtain a little more each day.

Cigarettes, pipes, cigars
Smoke and nicotine are damaging and tobacco is lethal to birds. It is therefore best not to smoke near your birds. Air the room regularly (beware of draughts) and keep

cigarettes and other tobacco products out of the bird's reach.

Poison
Parrots can get ill or die through tin, tobacco, zinc, glue, cleaning products and insecticides. Lead, plastic, ball pens, pens, alcohol, coffee and strong spices are also dangerous. Peanut shells are dangerous because of the aflatoxins. Remove all poisonous substances from the bird's surroundings or prevent it reaching them. Beware, for example, of lead bands in curtains. Do not give your birds twigs of poisonous trees or shrubs to chew on, such as honeysuckle, birch, acacia, holly, mountain elderberry, taxus or conifers. Do not let your bird eat houseplants.

Slender-billed Corella (Cacatua tenuirostris)

Lesser Vasa Parrot
*(Coracopsis
nigra)*

Houseplants

Several plants contain poisonous substances, which can be fatal for a bird. Poinsettia can be lethal if the bird eats a lot of it. Poisonous (but often very popular) houseplants are, among others, all Diefenbachia-species, oleander (Nerium oleander), goosefoot-plant, the great waxplant (Hoya carnosa), the poison nut plant (Stychnos nuxvomica) and the small periwinkle (Vinca minor). Cacti are dangerous due to their spikes, on which a bird can land by accident. Remove all poisonous plants before releasing your bird. Before buying new houseplants, inform yourself about whether they are poisonous to birds and possibly other pets.

Green-winged Macaw
(Ara chloroptera)

Fertilizer
Poisoning can also occur through eating fertilizer for houseplants. Especially if these fertilizers come as pellets, the parrot might have the tendency to eat them. This leads to nitrate poisoning.

Sharp objects
A parrot can injure itself on sharp objects, such as needles, spikes or

wood splinters. It may also swallow such objects. Do not leave anything lying around. When building a cage or an aviary, make sure that no splinters protrude on the inside.

Fruit
Most parrots love fruit and vegetables. You must limit them, of course, especially when it comes to the avocado. As mentioned above, avocados are extremely poisonous for parrots!

Changes in temperature
A parrot can catch a cold through extreme changes in temperature. Body parts can freeze through very low temperatures. Prevent this from happening: avoid sudden changes in temperature, check the heating in the indoor housing regularly and keep a watchful eye on parrots in an outdoor aviary in winter.

Jewellery
A parrot might swallow small beads, parts of earrings and other jewellery. Do not let your parrot play with your jewellery. This is also better for you or an unlucky visitor who suddenly has a parrot hanging on her earring.

St. Lucia Amazon
(Amazona versicolor)

Blue-eyed Cockatoo
(Cacatua ophthalmica)

Your parrot's behaviour

Green-winged
Macaw
(Ara chloroptera)

Instincts

Parrots are and will remain 'wild animals', however cute they are in the house. Your (living room) parrot is physically, psychologically and genetically identical to its 'family' in the wild, as no domestication of parrots has ever occurred.

Domestication means (very generally) conscious breeding with the intention of creating a species that displays a character or appearance appealing to humans. The most obvious example is dogs. They were bred for thousands of years by choosing individual animals with the desired characteristics for breeding, and avoiding others. There has been so much playing with the genetics of dogs that it is almost unbelievable that all the breeds, even a Jack Russell, have actually descended from the wolf, and that they all are one family.

It is different with parrots:
The Green-winged Macaw (Ara Chloroptera) and the Yellow-winged Macaw (Ara Macao) look very much alike. This is, however, not the result of genetic mutation (man-made). It is the result of using many captured animals and animals of the first captivity-bred generation in breeding. For domestication a lot of 'breed generations' are necessary so that the best puppies or chicks can be crossed and bred. There has not been enough time for this to happen with parrots.

Learning ability

There is a connection between instinct and intelligence in all animals. The stronger the instinct, the less it has to learn and therefore the less dependent it is on its parents. This is a very generalized conclusion, however. In parrots and other intelligent animals, many of the instinctive reactions are replaced by the ability to learn. They can adapt to changes in their environment and can generally cope better with unknown situations.

Parrot chicks are very dependent on their parents, and they have to be shown everything in order to learn. From eating to mating. It is, however, their learning ability and the lack of certain instincts, which have ensured that parrots have spread into the homes and hearts of people worldwide. Their lear-

ning ability also makes them difficult pets, as these intelligent birds understand immediately if things are wrong. This results in various forms of stress behaviour.

Support
Especially as parrots are such expensive pets, it is important to buy a bird from a breeder/dealer who understands his importance in the socialising process of the young bird. Breeders who understand the natural development of a young bird, and support it correctly, produce birds, which are happy, adapted and confident and less likely to develop behavioural problems. A parrot in the house is an important family member and it needs plenty of love and attention. Never forget that there is

Military Macaw
(Ara militaris)

Scarlet Macaw
(Ara macao)

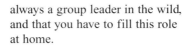

Blue-fronted
Amazon
(*Amazona aestiva*)

Salvin's Amazon
(*Amazona
autumnalis salvini*)

always a group leader in the wild, and that you have to fill this role at home.

Periods of learning

As parrots develop, they go through various stages. There are times when they are receptive to new lessons, for example about what is safe and what is not. During these periods, they also learn to adapt to changes and not see these as a threat. When they are grown, this consciousness has to remain activated for the bird to learn new things.

Behaviour and upbringing

Although parrots do not react primarily instinctively, they are also not completely programmable. The following is a list of fixed elements in parrot genes, which each parrot has, and behaviour with which every owner will be confronted.

A parrot is prey

A parrot is on the menu of other animals. Every parrot knows this dire reality as soon as it crawls out of the egg. A parrot in captivity will react aggressively to all disturbances from above and behind it. This can happen when a human approaches from behind without the parrot noticing, when you want to lift the bird up with a towel, or in the case of loud noises. Your parrot's back is extremely sensitive towards vibrations and changes in the air, such as would

occur when a hawk or eagle is attacking. Therefore always approach your parrot from the front and get young birds used to being picked up in a towel. Do not hang any suspended items above the cage, even if they are out of the parrot's reach.

A parrot experiences primarily visually

Nature has given prey animals certain means to survive (better). These adaptations are found everywhere in the animal (and plant) world. Think of the speed of the antelope, the camouflage of the chameleon and the quick reproduction rate of the mouse. Parrots are no exception. They have their eyes at the sides of their head, which makes their field of vision almost 360 degrees. They can see almost any predator approaching. As each eye sees independently, their vision does lose the sense of depth. This does not really matter, however, as a parrot takes on a defensive position once it sees an enemy approaching on the horizon.

Now that you know that your friend has an inherent fear of ending up as something else's lunch, you can use this knowledge to improve its life. Here are a few tips:
• Do not make any unexpected, abrupt movements when near the bird.
• Do not place the cage, aviary

Kea
(Nestor notabilis)

Red-bellied Parrot
(Poicephalus rufiventris)

and/or climbing tree next to a door or another spot where someone could suddenly appear. The best place for your parrot is opposite a door.

- Make a sound when approaching the bird (loud footsteps are usually sufficient).
- When approaching the bird in the dark, too, make a sound so that the bird can hear you approaching. Maybe leave a little night-lamp on.
- Parrots can react differently to various colours. They might even have a favourite colour, to which they are attracted. Colours can play a part when choosing a certain food.
- Eye contact is very important for parrots. Eye contact with you is very calming for your bird. Look at it when vacuum cleaning, phoning or similar.
- When becoming used to a new bird, look away slightly, so that it does not feel threatened by your stare. You can first work on eye contact and, later, on physical contact.
- Parrots with a very 'aggressive' character are often captivated and fascinated by eye contact. When training such a bird, it is very important to maintain eye contact. A bird you are looking at will not bite you that quickly.

The parrot is a gregarious animal

Parrots live in groups, as this offers protection. As many parrots

are very colourful, it is very difficult for a predator to catch an individual animal from a big group flying up. Evolution has made parrots very sociable, group-bound animals. The group is very important. A parrot cannot look after itself for its whole life without the help of others. It is therefore important that you integrate a pet bird into your 'group' and involve it in many aspects of family life.

Your birds see everyone in their direct environment as part of their group - the family, other pets and sometimes even regular visitors. The rest does not count. A bird will not like everybody equally,

but it will also not be easily panicked by a member of its group. Anyone who thinks that birds do not accept other pets should ask someone who keeps birds and dogs. They will tell them that parrots often throw bits of food out of the cage for their furry friend.

The group mentality often raises questions, such as 'my macaw is really sweet to my family and me, but terrified of strangers. What can I do?' Answer: Nothing! How would you feel at the thought of being somebody else's lunch? This is how a parrot reacts to a stranger. The good news is that this behaviour can and must be overcome. A parrot that can accept

Blue-fronted Amazon
(Amazona aestiva)

new things is less likely to be traumatised and will develop more curiosity and confidence. New things can be toys and changes to the interior of the cage or aviary, food, people, known things and routines, but also your own hair colour or cut.

Your parrot trying to take control

Animals which live in groups, herds or packs are genetically programmed to try to take over the leadership once the present leader is showing signs of weakness. Although very little is known about the group life of the parrot, a few things are obvious.

Parrots and many cockatoos search for food on the ground, which makes them very vulnerable. These groups have guards. This is a very important function in the group and always has to be fulfilled. Birds that search for food in trees and shrubs also have guards. This is usually the bird sitting highest up in the tree, the one with the best unobstructed view. There is often a lot of squabbling and fighting attached to this function, which always goes to big, older and very experienced birds in the group.

This behaviour also influences the relationship with your pet bird in various ways. Take for example the principle of 'the highest bird in the tree'. A lot of people (particularly in America) keep a stepladder next to their bird's cage. If the bird becomes dominating, they will go a little higher on the ladder and the bird will be subdued immediately. If its eyes are often higher than yours, then it will think that it automatically has the 'top position' and therefore is the boss. This is also why you should not let your bird sit on your shoulder. As behavioural consultant Liz Wilson puts it: "You always see two things with pirates: they always have a parrot on their shoulder and an eye patch." If your bird does not understand the command 'up', is in season, aggressive or irritated, do not let it sit on your shoulder.

Parrots also need rules. There are obviously things that they may and may not do. This has to be transferred to the domestic situation. The best example is the parrot that has not had its wings clipped, and is allowed to fly throughout the house. This bird does not have to stay sitting anywhere, does not need you as a means of transport, and can make its own decisions. The reason for keeping the bird like this is 'to keep it in a life-like situation'. A three bedroom flat in Brighton is, however, not the same as the tropical rainforest around the Amazon. It is natural for a bird to have rules, clarity and limits to its independence. Clipping its wings makes these clear enough.

Yellow-headed Amazon *(Amazona ochropcephala oratrix)*

Yellow-crowned Amazon (Amazona ochropcephala xantholaema Marajó)

Red-tailed
Amazon
*(Amazona
brasiliensis)*

Scaly-naped
Amazon *(Amazona
mercenaria)*

Sally Blanchard has developed the theory of 'nurturing guidance' to neutralise a bird's natural yearning for leadership. The first rule is that your bird must accept you as the boss. If you only present yourself as the feeder and carer, but not as the leader, your bird will not get the necessary leadership. On the other hand, you must not show any negative expressions of dominance. Hitting, scaring, dropping or shaking a bird all threaten its sense of security. You need to assert yourself as the leader of the pack, but never let your bird lose its trust in you.

Besides clipping its wings, holding your bird below the level of your chest and strengthening the relationship, you have to teach it some simple commands. The most common ones are 'up' and 'down', in case you want to take your bird somewhere and set it down again. Every time your bird steps just a little way onto your hand when you say 'up', your authority is reinforced. It is surprising how easily commands work in neutralising aggression and dominant behaviour.

Another problem connected to leadership has to do with safety and protection. If your bird thinks that it is the boss, it automatically assumes that you are not and that you are also not in a position to protect it. Even worse: your bird will try to protect you! Birds that

know no rules can become emotional wrecks. They scream, pluck and bite. These birds feel very insecure, as they do not know what to do. They have not learned to take control over a semi-detached family home in suburbia, and they are terrified. It is obvious how much happier these birds become once their wings have been clipped, they have learned to sleep in their cage, follow rules and have learned some commands.

When a pet bird bites, it is usually due to anger or pain. It can also be in the process of taking over leadership of its human companions or it may be in season. Let your bird know, in a firm but friendly way, that biting is not allowed.

**Parrots are emotional
and sensitive**
Parrots have their moods, but they are also very sensitive to the energy flows and the moods of the people around them. This is very important to know. It might happen that you feel like stroking your bird, while it is really not in the mood. This is the difference between a parrot and a dog. Dogs are (generally) much kinder and easier going. If you cannot easily see your parrot's mood, it will make this very clear and very quickly. By treating a parrot like a dog, you will teach it to bite. Parrots do not naturally bite, and

they try to avoid it. If you forget that your parrot is not a dog, do not notice that it does not feel like cuddling, do not notice its warning or that it is trying to escape, or do not even notice its verbal protest, then the bird cannot but bite. Once it notices that biting works, it is very difficult to stop this habit. Therefore, always observe your bird's behaviour, and respect its moods.

Your own mood, too, plays an important role. Parrots are very sensitive to it. When you are too late for a meeting, come storming into the room with your coat half on screaming 'up, up, in your cage', your parrot will be either be terrified, or it will play a game with you. Go out of the room, count to ten and enter the room again. Ask the bird calmly to step onto your hand, put it in its cage and leave the room calmly again. It always works!

Energy flows influence each other. Concentrate and keep your bird under control with your own energy. The more relaxed you are, the more relaxed your bird is. Therefore, do not panic if your bird plucks itself. Go to a bird vet's and have the problem and the causes analysed. There is no point in getting obsessed with your bird's obsessive behaviour. This works the other way round. Try to relax in the knowledge that you are doing everything in your

power with expert help. Let your behaviour convey this calmness to the bird.

All birds are noisy
Vocal communication is very important for birds and other sociable animals. If you have a bird with considerable volume, expect to hear it on a regular basis. If Mother Nature had not intended them to use their voice, she would not have given it to the parrots. This does not mean that you should not stop the screaming for attention. You should not, however, try to stop 'babble' at dawn and dusk, or the happiness expressed when welcoming you home. You can try to limit it, but it must not be suppressed, as this causes resistance.

Cape Parrot
(Poicephalus
robustus)

Military Macaw
(Ara militaris)

Blue and
Yellow Macaw
(Ara ararauna)

Bathing and showering are necessary

Bathing and/or showering are necessary for the physical and mental well-being of your bird. A bird that does not want to shower, has not learned this, has not been raised in an environment encouraging curiosity and investigation, or has experienced a trauma later on. A bird is scared by anything it does not know. Let it get used to a plant sprayer, a shallow bath, a tap or a shower. Beware of the risk of a wet bird catching a cold because of draughts.

Parrots are active animals

In the wild, parrots are busy for hours flying, playing and chewing on twigs, trees, pods, fruit, seeds and anything else they can reach. They do this for both feeding and fun. In captivity, all they have to do is go to the feed bowl. It is therefore important to furnish a big cage or an aviary with various perches, toys and twigs to tear apart. Maybe you could also put another play stand or a climbing tree outside the cage. A pet bird that does not play, must learn this, as it otherwise suppresses natural behaviour, which is not good.

Green-winged Macaw
(*Ara chloroptera*)

Parrots are mucky pups

Where parrots live becomes very obvious when you look at the floor - one big mess. Pods, seeds, pieces of twigs and other things are strewn all around. Parrots in the wild are one of the causes for new forest growth, as it is their 'task' to chew. It is in their genes. Chewing is something you have to accept and can keep in control with a vacuum cleaner, mop and broom. Do not try to break this habit. Birds have to shred, crumble and spill their food as much as they like.

Intelligence

Besides the instincts we discussed above, which each parrot has, they are simply intelligent! It seems obvious, but it is something that you have to bear in mind. Besides their desire for security, their intelligence plays a big role in all their behaviour.

Yourbehaviour

Ducorps' Cockatoo
(Cacatua ducorpsii)

Red-vented
Cockatoo
(Cacatua
haematuropygia)

Remember that:
• Parrots have a reason to do something (logic).
• Parrots want to be challenged with toys, chewing material, involvement in the family, and so on. Most parrots love to learn tricks, behaviour or words. They have, however, the concentration of a young, neurotic bundle of nerves, therefore do not make learning sessions too long or boring. Learning has to be fun.
• Parrots are just as keen to analy-

se and watch you as the other way round.
• Parrots can get confused when learning too much. Keep signals, commands and other messages as simple and clear as possible.

It is the right combination between instincts and intelligence that makes parrots so interesting. You must never forget, however, that they are wild animals with certain characteristics. You must recognize, acknowledge and

appreciate them. And think about it - when does it happen that a wild animal approaches you and demands to be cuddled.

Old age

Macaws and other big parrots are known to be tough birds, which can live to a very old age. The life expectancy of a macaw is considered to be 60 years and more. Not much has been documented on the life expectancy and ageing process of macaws and parrots.

Cuban Amazon
(Amazona
leucocephala)

Parrot Jungle in Miami, Florida, has done some research among its 'senior macaws' of 25 years and older. The results show that old age comes with the following complaints in macaws:
• cataracts, whereby they slowly become totally blind
• stiffness of the joints
• changes in skin colour and elasticity
• muscle weakness and weight loss
• gout
• moles, polyps, wart-like bumps on the skin of head and feet

It was striking that physical ageing started in this research group of macaws after the reproduction period. The reproductive cycle in macaws starts at about four years of age and ends at about 35 years. As soon as macaws can no longer reproduce, the complaints start.

Hawk-headed
Parrot
(Deroptyus
accipitrinus)

Breeding with your parrots

When keeping several birds of the same species, the question arises whether you want to breed with them.

If you have very special, rare birds, you are actually obliged to at least create the right environment for these birds to breed to ensure the continuing existence of this species. Pedigrees or 'EEPs' have been created for many of these endangered birds, in which you can participate.

Putting a couple together

Creating a pair that like each other is the first point to think about. This small book cannot go into detail about all the things to consider. Putting a couple together often means adapting the caging. Pairs of big parrots need at least an (indoor) aviary, with one or more nesting boxes. A nesting box can be made of a tree trunk, this is called a 'natural nesting box'. You can also buy ready-made wooden nesting boxes. The size depends on the size of the birds. It is also possible to make a nesting box yourself. You can read more about this in books about keeping and looking after parrots.

If the couple you put together like each other and are mating, they will need humidity, feeding, nesting material and rest. In some species, only the mother broods; in others it is a shared task. Sometimes the male joins the mother in the nesting box and feeds her. The hen only comes out to discharge of a lot of excretion at once and maybe to quickly drink something. Otherwise, she keeps the eggs warm and turns them regularly. The couple can get very aggressive during the whole brooding period, even if they were usually very tame. The brooding period varies from 20 to 30 days and the young then hatch within one to three days, including pauses.

Good parent animals will feed and raise their young themselves. This is the best that can happen. If this does not happen, you have to assess the seriousness of the situation and maybe take the young away. Depending on the chicks' age, this is very difficult. Fortunately, you can now buy ready-made chick feed, which you prepare by adding boiling water. It

Kea young
(Nestor notabilis)

Senegal Parrot young bird
(Poicephalus senegalus)

still remains a big job to raise the young parrots. Your babies need to be ringed with a seamless closed identification ring so that the country of origin can be determined. Depending on the species, you have to take action as prescribed by the CITES-bureau.

Breeding account

Under the BUDEP law and the CITES-bureau, which reinforces this law, you are obliged to keep a 'breeding account'. When asked, you have to prove where your birds are from, which ring numbers they have, which chicks they have bred, where they have gone to, and so on.

This account can easily be kept in a notebook or a shoebox, but there are also software programs available, with which you can keep it on a computer. You can make the account as detailed as you wish, and you can even add medical records or any prizes won to each bird's account.

Breeding programmes

International breeding programmes have been created for endangered parrot breeds. Individuals, zoos and bird parks, which keep a certain species, participate in these. At European level, an inventory of birds in captivity is made and ways are sought to mate individual birds. This helps the particular species to survive. The breeding programmes are associa-

ted with the term EEP, European, Endangered Species Breeding Program. These EEPs not only include parrots, but all sorts of exotic endangered species. Breeding programmes operate not only on a European level but on an even wider scale. The thought behind these programmes is always the same: the survival of the species in the wild by optimum breeding in captivity and, where at all possible, reintroduction of the species into their original habitat.

Young parrots: African Grey Congo and Blue-Fronted Amazon

Brown-headed Parrot *(Poicephalus cryptoxanthus)*

Parrot species

There are more than 300 parrot species, and they vary in length from ten centimetres (dwarf parrots) to one metre (macaw).

Salmon-crested Cockatoo (Cacatua moluccensis)

They also vary from 'boring' to very colourful and from quiet to very mobile and playful. Parrots can become very old. Parakeets and lovebirds can easily become teenagers, and macaws, amazons and cockatoos can become 60 or older. The African parrots, amazons, macaws and cockatoos belong to the 'large parrot species'. We have made an overview to give you some idea of characteristics, appearance and behaviour. Of course, exceptions confirm the rule.

Cockatoos

Cockatoos originate in Indonesia, New Guinea and Australia. They vary from 30 cm (Goffin's Cockatoo) to about 55 cm (Salmon-Crested Cockatoo and Palm Cockatoo). All cockatoos

share one characteristic: their crest. Some species have a crest that is always visible, even when lying flat to the head. Examples are the large, medium and small Sulphur-Crested Cockatoo. Other cockatoos have a smaller crest, which is not visible when the bird is resting. This is the case with the Goffin's Cockatoo, the Bare-Eyed Cockatoo and the Philippine Cockatoo. When cockatoos are irritated or excited, or when they want to impress others, the crest is raised.

Cockatoos are often regarded as the clowns amongst the parrot family. As soon as they wake up, they begin to play and they only stop when they go to sleep. They play with food, toys, twigs, with each other or with humans around them. They are also real acrobats. They love to hang underneath bars, ropes or twigs and they also perform all sorts of tricks. Screws and locks are not safe from their strong beak. They observe exactly how you open the doors and, sooner than you think, they can open them as quickly as you shut them. They chew on everything. Therefore always ensure that fresh twigs are available in the cage or aviary. Cockatoos do not differentiate between a cherry twig you have given them and your fine cherry-wood furniture. It is therefore important that you always offer them something to destroy.

Electus Parrots

The various varieties of Electus Parrot also originate in the area of New Guinea, Indonesia and Cape York (Australia). Most species are named after the area where they originate, such as the Halmahera and the Solomon Parrot. The difference between male and female is very obvious with the Electus Parrots. The males are mostly green; the females are brilliantly red with a blue sheen. Depending on the sub-species, they have various shades or extra colours. Electus Parrots can be quiet, kind-natured birds, but they do have a loud volume. They are nowhere near as destructive as cockatoos.

Macaws

Macaws run the show in bird parks and zoos. The beautiful colours are the most obvious characteristic of the macaw. Add an impressive beak and an accompanying volume, and the image of the bird is easily formed. They are, however, normally quiet and good-natured birds, which need a big aviary or flight. If they are housed in too small a space, they often damage their (tail) feathers on the bars or pluck themselves due to boredom.

There are small dwarf macaws or the bigger macaws. The bigger species can reach a length of one metre, including the tail. Luckily, individuals now breed more macaws in captivity, including the Blue Macaw. This means that it is unnecessary to catch them in the wild and import them. There is plenty of offspring available. Some macaw species belong to the very endangered species. This is the case for the Hyacinth Macaw, Lear's Macaw and Spix's Macaw. Only approximately 40 Spix's Macaws are known of in captivity. Only one individual (a male) lives in Brazil in the wild. An international rescue project has been started for this species, where all possible effort is being made to prevent the Spix's Macaw from becoming extinct in the wild.

Amazons

As the name indicates, amazons originate in South America. They are spread over a large area, which includes large parts of South and

Eclectus Parrot:
left: female,
right: male
(Eclectus roratus)

Spix's Macaw
(Cyanopsitta spixii)

Spix's Macaw
(Cyanopsitta spixii)

Central America. Some sub-species, however, have only a very small area of distribution. This is due to natural barriers, nesting opportunities and the availability of food. All the amazon species (approximately 27) share one characteristic, which is the colour green over a large part of their coat. Besides green, they have other colours, which depend on the (sub)species. The Yellow-faced Amazon and the Greater Yellow-faced Amazon have a lot of yellow on their head. Other colours common with amazons are orange, red, blue, purple and white, in all sorts of nuances and combinations.

The sizes of Amazons range from just under 30 centimetres (Cuban Amazon and White-fronted Amazon) to about 45 centimetres (for example the rare Imperial Amazon). This depends on the species, the sex and the area of origin. Males are often a little more strongly built than females, but exceptions prove the rule here, too.

Many amazons become good talkers or imitators of all sorts of sounds, depending on the species and the individual. The Blue-fronted Amazon and the Yellow-fronted Amazon are good talkers, but this does not guarantee success. To get a bird to talk, whistle and/or sing you must spend hours every day with your bird. This is not, however, a guarantee that your darling will say whatever you want it to do. They often find screeching doors, phones ringing, door bells and barking dogs far more interesting. Or they stick to typical bird sounds.

The Pionus varieties or "Red-Tailed Parrots", too, come from South America. These are pretty, friendly cage and aviary birds as long as they feel at home. Most Pionus varieties are not too large but their ability to talk is limited.

African parrots

These include the Timneh Grey Parrot, the Meyer's parrot, the Senegal Parrot and the Congo Grey Parrot. The Grey Parrot is often found in living rooms, where it is a sociable and valued member of the family. It is famous for its ability to imitate, but this is not a guarantee. It is an 'easy' bird to breed, which means that there is plenty of offspring on offer. Grey Parrots born in captivity are usually very affectionate, playful, eager to learn and quiet, although there are notorious screamers among them. Grey Parrots are very sensitive to stress, which is often expressed in plucking their own plumage. This can also be a sign of boredom.

Reintroduction to the wild

There are programs worldwide to reintroduce birds, which have been raised in captivity, into their original wild habitats. These projects often take years. A great deal of research is done into the environment, the factors which caused the extinction of the animals (such as availability of food, natural enemies and the influence of man), suitable

individuals for reproduction, and so on.

Reintroduction to the wild might seem preferable to breeding in captivity, but sadly not all birds can be reintroduced to the wild. Man is often the cause for the extinction of certain parrot species. Increasing urbanisation, the felling of the rainforest for the building of roads and the production of timber, nest robbery, and tourism - these are all influences, which drastically restrict the habitat and reproduction of parrots. This is why breeding programmes for parrots in captivity are a valuable addition to the survival of exotic species.

Jardine's Parrot
(Poicephalus gulielmi)

Senegal Parrot
(Poicephalus senegalus)

Your parrot's health

A parrot can live a very long time. Whether or not a parrot reaches old age depends on many factors.

Its feeding, housing, hereditary disposition and luck all play a role, of course. Health issues, too, need your attention, if you want to enjoy your parrot, cockatoo, amazon or macaw for a long time to come. We have already mentioned all the points that are important when buying a parrot. You can, however, be confronted with a number of illnesses or situations, in which you need to give first aid.

The following list is by no means complete, but it gives you some guidance for some more common ailments. Luckily, there are many very good vets, and also an increasing number of specialised bird vets. They are always there to help, not only in the case of illness or accident, but also to give advice about related issues, such as feeding, housing and behaviour.

Acting

A bird will try to hide its condition for as long as possible, even from you. This is in its blood: a parrot cannot show that it is sick in the wild. It would be easy prey for its natural enemies. It has to and will stay with the group. This instinct is in every parrot, and it will try to appear as fit and healthy as possible in front of people. It is therefore important to observe your bird regularly when it is not watching you. You can then check whether there is anything wrong with it. Signs are sitting with raised feathers, panting, sitting on the ground instead of on a perch, or excessive sleep.

Common illnesses
Polyomavirus
This is a virus that is found worldwide and causes many problems in parrots and parakeets. Especially macaws, Electus Parrots, Lovebirds, Budgerigars and Caiques are vulnerable to it. The virus causes illness especially in young birds. The older the bird when infected, the less serious the illness is. Adult birds often do not become ill when infected with Polyoma. They can, however, be carriers of the virus and therefore infect other birds. Infection occurs via feeding the young or via material from the feathers and/or dried faeces.

Symptoms: slow growth process and slow emptying of the crop. A young bird is suspect if it has bleeding under the skin or loses more than a drop of blood when it plucks a feather. Young birds ready to fly out are suspect if the wing and tail feathers do not develop properly. They cannot fly and are called 'crawlers'.

A vaccine is available, although it is not yet officially approved in all countries. Check with your vet.

Beak- and Feather disease
This virus attacks the bird's immune system. Just as with Polyoma, the virus can be in the system for years before the bird becomes ill. In both the cases, infected birds might appear com-

pletely healthy again after three months, but both illnesses are also very difficult to treat. As Beak- and Feather disease spreads via feathers and faeces, it is very important that a sick bird is recognised and isolated as quickly as possible.

Symptoms: it is often difficult to recognise this disease. Especially young birds die within a few days or weeks without showing the feather abnormalities so typical of this disease. This form of the disease is particularly common with cockatoos and Grey parrots. With birds, which become ill when the first feathers develop, these are affected straight away. This is often combined with vomiting, diarrhoea and lethargy. The beak and claws may also be affected. This usually starts with the upper beak. The horn becomes softer and paler in colour and splits, and tumours can develop, which can reach into the beak. The internal damage of this disease is more serious than the external symptoms. Many birds with Beak- and Feather disease die within six to twelve months after the disease has manifested itself. They die of secondary infections as their immune system is very weak. If the secondary infections are treatable, the bird may survive a long time. Especially budgerigars and lovebirds with Beak- and Feather disease can live for several years.

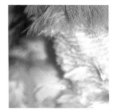

The disease can be diagnosed by different methods. The surest method is a blood test. There is, however, no vaccine available yet, although some promising research is being done in Australia.

Paramyxo virus
The family of Paramyxo viruses is very large and divided into nine groups.

One virus from group nine is called Newcastle disease, is found worldwide and can affect many birds and mammals (including humans). Newcastle disease has also been diagnosed with parrots. Especially Falcon Parakeets, Amazons, Plum-headed Parakeets and Electus Parrots are receptive to this virus. The virus spreads via faeces and saliva and can damage various organs in the body. The symptoms are therefore manifold. Both young and old animals can be affected.

Symptoms: most sick animals display respiratory problems and diarrhoea. Some animals also show nervous symptoms (twisting the neck, trembling). These cases usually die, sometimes after months. If a bird does not show symptoms 30 days after being exposed to the virus (at a show, for example), the chance is very small that it will become ill. The animal can carry the virus and infect others. Rosellas are particularly known for this. Vaccination

is possible, but the law only allows it in exceptional cases. This means that the animal must be in a life-threatening condition. The vaccination gives protection lasting between a few months and a year. General hygiene and regular cleaning with a chlorine solution help to kill the virus in the surroundings.

Paramyxo viruses of group three cause the "twisted neck syndrome". The virus can attack the pancreas in some breeds (Grey parrots, for example). Increased excretion is a symptom of this condition. The faeces may also be lighter in colour and greasy to putty-like in consistency. The mortality rate of animals with twisted neck syndrome varies. Newcastle disease is far less common with parrots than twisted neck syndrome.

Psittacosis
This is caused by the Chlamydia bacterium. Chlamydia psittaci is highly contagious for many birds and mammals, such as horses, cattle, sheep, deer and humans, too. Chlamydia psittaci causes psittacosis, which is also called parrot disease. The disease is spread via feather material and dried faeces of sick birds.

Symptoms: the outer signs vary with this disease, too. They include respiratory distress, coughing, spitting, pus-like excretion from the nose, clamping tight an eye,

Yellow-headed
Amazon

Yellow-lored
Amazon (Amazona
xantholora)

light-green excretion of diarrhoea or yellow urea. It often takes weeks before an infected animal shows symptoms. Parrots can also be carriers without suffering themselves. Infected parrots, ducks and chickens cause most, and the most serious, symptoms in humans. A human with psittacosis has flu-like symptoms, such as high temperature, serious headache, shivering, shortness of breath and drowsiness. If the illness is not diagnosed and treated, pneumonia, meningitis, liver and kidney damage can occur. Psittacosis

is easy to treat with antibiotics. The treatment of a sick human or animal takes several weeks.

Illnesses which can be transferred to humans
Besides Newcastle disease and Psittacosis, there are several other illnesses that can be transferred from birds to humans. They include salmonella, tuberculosis, campylobacteriosis and influenza C. It would be too much to discuss all these illnesses in detail here. It is advisable for you as a bird owner to bear in mind that you can catch

diseases from your birds. This can be important information for your GP!

First Aid with birds

A lot of problems need the help of specialists, of course, but it is good to be able to recognise certain illnesses and problems. In some cases, first aid given by the owner is both possible and important. In the following, we introduce a number of conditions with which a bird owner might be confronted.

Fractures and broken bones

Broken bones are very common with birds. They can be in a foot, a wing, the sternum or in the skull. Calcium deficiency can cause broken bones in young birds, or it can cause the bones to grow so crooked that they have to be broken and straightened. This is very common among young Grey parrots. Sufficient calcium is the first requirement.

Broken bones can be treated in several ways, some of which you can do at home. The first possibility is a splint, which means that a supporting slat is used with a bandage wrapped around it.

Bandaging is another possibility. This means that a tight, but not too tight, bandage is wrapped around the fracture. The wing or foot is fixed against the body. The bandage is wrapped around the

foot or wing and the body. The bandage has to be tight enough to let the fracture heal, but it has to allow the bird to breathe without restriction. Young birds also need to be able to grow.

A third possibility of treating broken bones is surgery, during which a pin is placed in the fracture. This is very easy, as birds' bones are hollow and do not contain marrow. The thin, sterile pins can therefore be placed in the bone, and often do not need to be removed after healing. This surgery must be performed by a (bird specialist) vet.

A broken wing is far more complicated than a broken foot. The stabilising of a broken wing requires the utmost precision. It is also questionable whether a broken wing is ever fully usable again.

The nice thing about birds is that broken bones heal very quickly due to the good circulation in their bones. Three weeks rest and a splint, bandage or surgery is usually sufficient to heal a fracture.

Traumas and brain damage

A heavy blow, by flying hard against a window or mesh, for example, often causes a trauma, such as concussion, and can also cause internal bleeding. Outer signs include a tilted position of the head, and blindness in one eye. The bird might sit in a comatose state on the ground of the aviary.

In the case of not too serious concussion, the bird often recovers within a few hours. Mix dextrose into the water, and keep the bird in a separate, warm and dark cage. It is surprising how quickly birds can recover. If this does not happen, you need to contact your vet, and your bird will require more prolonged treatment and care.

Egg-binding

This is a problem every bird owner should be familiar with, as it can affect any hen and can be fatal if no action is taken. The hen prepares to lay an egg. The next day, there is still no egg and the

Hispaniolan Amazon
(*Amazona ventralis*)

bird is sitting on the nest trembling. You now have to immediately try to feel whether something is wrong with the egg. Do not wait any longer, as the egg can cause dehydration of the cloaca wall. The egg needs lubricant to be pushed to the outside, but by now it will be stuck to the cloaca wall. The urethra and the intestines also end in the cloaca. Due to the dehydration the bird cannot excrete. Serious problems occur within hours, which will be fatal.

It is important to check whether the bird still excretes and eats. If this is the case, the situation is not (yet) life threatening. Keep the bird separated and warm, to ensure that you can support and observe her carefully. If the bird does no longer excrete, you must massage salve or oil into the cloaca. Salve can be a little Vaseline or hand cream, for example. Oil can be olive oil, salad oil or similar. The salve or oils make the egg nice and smooth again and loosen it from the cloaca wall, so that the bird can try to push the egg out herself. It is best to keep the bird separated and warm for this. She is probably exhausted by all the pressing. The warmth will help her to regain strength, and you should also mix dextrose into the water. If the egg has not been laid after a few hours, other action needs to be taken, a caesarean, for example. You must leave this to an expert.

Prolapsed Cloaca

This means that part of the cloaca hangs outside the bird. This often occurs after a difficult laying and is generally not very serious. Usually the part that is hanging outside can be gently pushed back again with a cotton buds or a finger with some salve. It can become an emergency if the prolapse becomes damaged or a blockage occurs. Damage can occur if the bird sits against a perch or mesh with the prolapse. If blockage occurs, the prolapse becomes dark blue to violet and the bird must be taken to a vet straight away. Sometimes, the prolapse can be pushed back with a finger, but comes out again later. In this case, a visit to the vet's is advisable, and the prolapse will be surgically fastened.

Serious respiratory distress

This can have various causes, including bleeding, infection of the mucous membrane in the airway, vitamin-A deficiency, parasites, fungal infections or a rupture of the air pocket.

First aid cannot help with internal bleeding. Specialist help is also often useless. External bleedings can be stopped, of course. You can use a cornflour poultice for this as it stops bleeding very efficiently, or a burning cigarette, with which you can cauterise the wound. The advantage of cauterising is that it kills all the bacteria.

Black Cockatoo (Calyptorhynchus funereus)

White-tailed Cockatoo (Calyptorhynchus f. baudinii)

We will now only discuss the fungal infections as other causes of respiratory distress. Young birds can catch a fungal infection from an infected nesting box or a parent animal. The solution is to thoroughly clean the nesting box, disinfect or change it. If the chick caught the infection from a parent bird, this also needs to be treated.

(Young) parrots normally cope well with a small amount of fungus in their environment. When their defence system is weakened, however, a fungal infection can lead to problems in the young bird. It can no longer fight the infection and seems short of breath. It is important to notice early signs of respiratory problems, so that the fungi can be treated with an anti-fungal solution early on. Once the infection has spread to the air sacks, so-called sprayers need to be used. Once a bird has collected a lot of fungus in its body, no more can be done.

Uraemia

If a bird eats too much protein (usually via too much egg-food), it can no longer get rid of its waste products, the urea. Kidney gout and possibly uraemia are the result. A visible symptom is increased thirst. This can be a sign of kidney and intestinal problems. There is no first aid solution.

Shock

This means that the parrot falls into a coma. Do not try to treat this yourself. Keep the bird dark and warm, and take it to the vet's. Solutions include a cortisone injection, an infusion with liquid and (if necessary) force-feeding. Once the bird feels better, you should keep it in the light for 24 hours, so that it gets the best possible opportunity to eat, drink and regain its strength.

Bite wounds

A lot of birds are bitten by other pets, such as dogs, cats, guinea pigs and the like. This is often lethal as these pets can spread Pasteurella infection via their saliva. Birds are particularly vulnerable.

Poisoning

Poisoning can occur via inhalation, ingestion or intoxication. Inhalation includes the inhalation of poisonous gasses and vapours, such as Vapona and the gasses that are released when a Teflon pan burns. Ingestion means that the bird eats something poisonous. Parrots can also die of mouse poison nowadays, as this poison works faster now than it did in the past. The mouse might manage to run after eating the poison and end up in the aviary, where it eventually dies. A lot of parrots love to nibble at dead mice and thus come in contact with the strong poison, which is also dangerous to birds. Intoxication can also be by heavy metals, for example by eating the lead thread in curtains or nibbling at a window in a lead frame.

Damaged feathers

Wing quills can break off or be bitten off. The remaining stumps need to be removed (under anaesthetic). A bird without quills no longer moults, so this problem does not solve itself.

Parrots that start plucking themselves indoors might do this because the humidity is too low. Especially in winter, birds are often placed in a nice warm spot. The central heating causes the humidity to drop very low, which causes problems with the birds' feathers. Daily spraying with lukewarm water and a bath can solve the problem. An air moistener is also an advisable addition.

Blue-headed Parrot
(Pionus menstruus)

Sole and foot damage

A 'bumblefoot' is a condition where there are tumours under the soles of the feet. These can be caused by injury, by pressure

sores from sitting all the time on the same artificial perch or by self-mutilation. It can often be solved by thorough cleaning of the foot, application of an oint- ment and bandaging. In other cases, surgery is necessary.

To prevent 'sitting sores', it is advisable to use natural twigs as perches in the cage or aviary. Just saw thick branches to the right size and place them in the cage. These branches will vary in hard- ness, surface and circumference and therefore minimize the chance of sitting sores. The feet are con- stantly stimulated.

Crop damage

When raising young birds by hand, it can happen that the gruel is given too hot. A hole in the crop occurs, through which the food comes out again. This requi- res immediate intervention by a vet. The burnt tissue is removed and the healthy tissue is brought together. Luckily, the crop skin is elastic enough to stretch to its normal size within days.

Here is some advice: Gruel should be given too cold rather than too hot. And always be careful with microwaveable food. This is often hotter in the bottom of the bowl than on top. When checking microwaveable food, stir it well first to ensure that the gruel has the right temperature throughout.

Sick bay

It is advisable to always have a 'sick bay cage' available. This does not have to be a major investment. A so-called guinea pig cage with a plastic upper and a hole, over which you can hang a 40-watt lamp, is sufficient. It does not need any perches, as by sitting on perches, a sick bird only wastes the energy that is so important for its recovery. Put lots of bowls with nice food and drink in the cage, which encourage it to eat and drink.

Put only newspaper on the floor, so that you can easily check the faeces. Mix some honey or dex- trose into the water. A high dosa- ge of a vitamin A and B complex is ideal. If necessary, you might have to force-feed the patient via a crop catheter. This speeds up recovery. The vet can lay an infu- sion, as fluids are vital. Keep the bird as quiet as possible, so that it can recover.

Yellow-headed
Amazon *(Amazona
ochropcephala oratrix)*

Another general rule: A bird that does not eat is sick, but a bird that does not drink is even sicker. This bird needs to be given fluids in one way or another to keep its kidneys working.

Tips for parrots

Pesquet's Parrot
(Psittrichas fulgidus)

- To keep and breed birds in a responsible manner is an art.
- Do not buy an imported bird, which has been caught in the wild. Plenty of birds bred in captivity are available.
- Avocado is extremely poisonous for birds!
- It is important to name birds by their correct Latin name to prevent confusion.
- Do not buy your birds at the first opportunity. Visit as many breeders in your area as possible.
- Do not buy a chick that still needs to be fed gruel.
- A parrot can get very old. Does this fit into your future plans?
- Birds need daily care.

- The bigger the cage or aviary, the better.
- Draughts are fatal for birds. Prevent them!
- Attention, toys, optimum care, plenty of space. These are a few of the demands that your bird has of you.
- A parrot is intelligent. Stimulate this and remember games, tricks and commands.
- Water, showering, spraying or bathing are a 'must' for every bird.
- A bird that is not eating is sick, but a bird that is not drinking is even sicker.
- Only buy young and ringed birds.

Names

**The names in English and
Latin popular parrots.**

English name	Latin name
Blue-fronted Amazon	*Amazona aestiva*
Red-lored Parrot	*Amazona autumnalis*
Yellow-headed Amazon	*Amazona ochrocephala*
Cuban Parrot	*Amazona leucocephala*
Orange-winged Amazon	*Amazona amazonica*
White-fronted Amazon	*Amazona albifrons*
Electus parrot	*Eclectus roratus*
Blue and gold Macaw	*Ara ararauna*
Greenwing Macaw	*Ara chloroptera*
Scarlet Macaw	*Ara macao*
Great green Macaw	*Ara ambigua*
Chestnut-fronted Macaw	*Ara severa*
Hyacinth Macaw	*Anodorhynchus hyacinthinus*
Spix's Macaw	*Cyanopsitta spixii*
Sulphur-crested Cockatoo	*Cacatua galerita*
White-crested Cockatoo	*Cacatua alba*
Salmon-crested Cockatoo	*Cacatua moluccensis*
Long-billed corella	*Cacatua tenuirostris*
Goffin's Cockatoo	*Cacatua goffini*
Major Mitchell's Cockatoo	*Cacatua leadbeateri*
Red tailed black-Cockatoo	*Calyptorhynchus banksii*
Palm Cockatoo	*Probosciger aterrimus*
Rose-breasted Cockatoo	*Eolophus roseicapillus*
Cape Parrot	*Poicephalus robustus*
Meyer's Parrot	*Poicephalus meyeri*
Senegal Parrot	*Poicephalus senegalus*
Jardine Parrot	*Poicephalus gulielmi*
Congo grey Parrot	*Psittacus erithacus*
African grey Parrot	*Psittacus erithacus timneh*
Blue-headed Pionus	*Pionus menstruus*
Bronze-winged Pionus	*Pionus chalcopterus*
White-crowned Pionus	*Pionus senilis*
Black-headed Parrot	*Pionites melanocephala*
White-belly Caique	*Pionites leucogaster*
Kea	*Nestor notabilis*

Other books from About Pets

Key features of the series are:
- Most affordable books
- Packed with hands-on information
- Well written by experts
- Easy to understand language
- Full colour original photography
- 70 to 110 photos
- All one needs to know to care well for their pet
- Trusted authors, veterinary consultants, breed and species expert authorities
- Appropriate for first time pet owners
- Interesting detailed information for pet professionals
- Title range includes books for advanced pet owners and breeders
- Includes useful addresses, veterinary data, breed standards.